BAR CHART BASICS

DARRELL R. JOBMAN

SuperCharts Disk Included

TRADE SECRETS

Bar Chart
BASICS
BIG RETURNS USING BAR CHARTS

DARRELL R. JOBMAN
FOREWORD BY TOM BIEROVIC

This book, along with other books, are available at discounts that make it realistic to provide them as gifts to your customers, clients, and staff. For more information on these long lasting, cost effective premiums, please call John Boyer at 800-424-4550 or email him at john@traderslibrary.com.

ISBN 1-883272-23-8

Printed in the United States of America.

CONTENTS

FOREWORD

Trading the world's financial markets may be the perfect business opportunity for the twenty-first century entrepreneur. You can trade from home and live anywhere in the world you choose. You will have a lower start-up cost and lower overhead expenses than in almost any other business. All you'll need is a computer, software, and some trading capital. You can set your own schedule, trading when you want to and taking time off when you want to. You can run your trading business with no inventory, no employees, no customers, no lawsuits or complaints, and no bureaucratic interference. It's just you and the markets you trade. Most importantly, your results are based solely on your own skill and effort. If you learn to trade well, you will enjoy potentially unlimited income for the rest of your life. You can even pass your favorite winning trading systems down to your children and grandchildren!

Understanding the bar chart is the starting point for learning how to analyze the markets. In *Bar Chart Basics*, Darrell Jobman presents a clear, concise introduction to bar charts. He covers a myriad of useful topics in this compact little booklet. From trendlines and chart patterns to gaps and retracements, Jobman explains what you need to know to profit from bar charts.

After you've become proficient in reading bar charts, you may want to add other elements of technical analysis to your

repertoire. Moving averages and momentum oscillators repre-
sent the next logical step in your study of technical analysis.

Moving averages smooth price data to make the underlying
trend easier to identify. Chart 1 shows a daily bar chart with a
50-day simple moving average. If you connect the daily closes,
the resulting line is very erratic. Note, however, that the 50-
day simple moving average in Chart 1 is very smooth. It only
changes direction twice, turning up in June and down in
September. When the moving average is rising, the trend is
bullish; when it's declining, the trend is bearish. The position
of closing prices relative to the moving average is another way
to use moving averages to determine the trend. If the current
close is above the moving average, the trend is up; if the current close is below the moving average, the trend is down.

CHART 1— DAILY BAR CHART
SOURCE: OMEGA RESEARCH

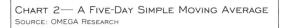

CHART 2— A FIVE-DAY SIMPLE MOVING AVERAGE
SOURCE: OMEGA RESEARCH

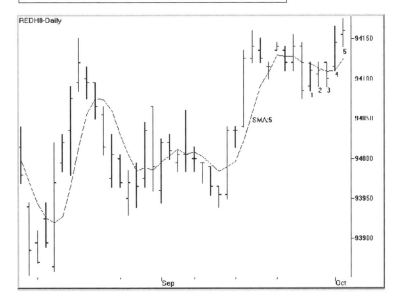

Chart 2 shows a five-day simple moving average. Note that the most recent five closes are numbered 1 - 5. To calculate the moving average, add the five closes and divide the total by 5. Also note that the five-day moving average in Chart 2 is not as smooth as the 50-day moving average in Chart 1. A fast moving average (like a five-day) generally changes direction more frequently, stays nearer to closing prices, and smooths the data less than does a slow moving average (like a 50-day).

One way to trade with a moving average is to buy when prices close above the moving average and to sell when prices close below the moving average. Chart 3 shows that trading with a moving average works well when a market is in a strong trend (either up or down) but that it performs poorly when a market is choppy.

CHART 3— TRADING WITH A MOVING AVERAGE
SOURCE: OMEGA RESEARCH

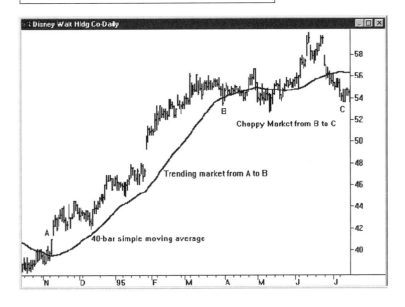

In today's fast-moving markets, many traders focus more on a market's momentum than its long-term trend. Rather than waiting for a trend to change from down to up, for example, they buy when the downtrend begins to lose its bearish momentum. Usually a change in momentum does precede a change in price, just as a ball that you throw into the air will attain its maximum upward momentum when it leaves your hand and will gradually lose momentum until it finally begins to fall. Although the laws of physics are much more reliable than any theories or indicators we apply to the financial markets, the study of momentum definitely has a place in the trader's toolbox.

An example of a momentum indicator is the Relative Strength Index (RSI for short). Chart 4 shows a daily bar chart with a nine-day RSI beneath it. Like all other oscillators, RSI measures the market's momentum - the acceleration or deceleration of price changes - in an attempt to anticipate a change in trend. RSI overbought and oversold levels are usually drawn at 70 and 30 or 80 and 20. An overbought market may have risen too far too fast, and an oversold market may have fallen too far too fast. A market with the RSI at an overbought or oversold extreme may be past due for a consolidation, a correction, or a trend reversal.

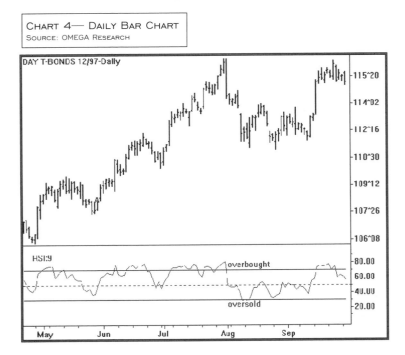

CHART 4— DAILY BAR CHART
SOURCE: OMEGA RESEARCH

After you've studied bar charts, moving averages, and momentum oscillators, you might want to develop your own trading system. I believe that trading in a systematic manner is much more likely to produce consistent profits than by trading in a discretionary, by-the-seat-of-your-pants manner where trades are based on intuition, hot tips, or the daily news.

There are at least six benefits of systematic trading.

1. You can design a system that is compatible with your own personality and trading style - a system that you are comfortable with.

2. You will eliminate overly emotional trading and reduce the stress of constantly making subjective, spur-of-the-moment trading decisions.

3. You will have objective entry and exit criteria that have been validated by historical testing of quantifiable data, thus increasing your confidence and strengthening your ability to trade in a highly disciplined manner.

4. You will have a method for controlling risk.

5. You will know when and where to get out of a trade if the market goes against you.

6. You will know the maximum peak-to-valley drawdown that your system has experienced in the past, and you can make sure that you are adequately capitalized, both financially and psychologically, to withstand another worst-case drawdown.

Before you can develop your own trading system, you need to decide the markets, the timeframe, and the type of market activity you want to trade. Markets you can trade include stocks like American Airlines or Union Carbide, mutual funds like Fidelity Magellan or the Kaufmann Fund, physical commodities like soybeans or crude oil, and financial futures like Eurodollars or the S&P 500 Index. You can also trade options on stocks, commodities, and financial futures.

In addition to specializing in a particular kind of market, you'll probably want to concentrate on one particular timeframe, especially if you're just starting out as a trader. The timeframes you'll want to consider for your trading are weekly, daily, and intraday. Traders who are very busy with other full-time commitments and who don't want to spend a lot of their limited free time on the markets might choose to focus on the weekly timeframe. Weekly traders check their positions and new signals on the weekend and call in their orders before they go to work on Monday morning. Traders who want to become full-time professionals as soon as possible and who have the temperament and resources to follow and trade the markets all day might choose intraday timeframes like five, fifteen, and thirty minute periods.

Traders who concentrate on trading the daily bars fall in between the weekly traders and the intraday traders. If you are willing and able to devote at least a few hours of your time every evening to trading but don't want to have to follow the markets during the day, you might want to specialize in the daily timeframe.

Another important consideration as you plan your trading system is the type of market activity you are most interested in and most comfortable with. I divide price action into three basic categories: trending, non-trending, and volatile. A trending market is characterized by a large, sustained price advance or decline. A non-trending market moves sideways with smaller, "drifting" price swings up and down. A volatile market features sharp, quick price jumps. Each category of price action demands a corresponding type of trading system. You will want to specialize in one type of market activity, especially at first, and to design systems that perform well in that particular environment.

Once you've chosen the market, timeframe, and type of market activity you want to specialize in, your next task is to become very knowledgeable about set-ups, entries, and exits. Set-ups are the criteria you specify to alert you that a trading opportunity has developed. Set-ups don't get you into a trade; they do tell you that market conditions have become favorable for a trade. An example of a buy set-up is a market posting two consecutive closes above a moving average. An example of a sell set-up is RSI turning down from above 70.

An entry is the criterion that must be met after a set-up for a trade to be initiated. An example of a buy entry is a close above the two-day high. An example of a sell entry is a decline below the previous week's low.

An exit is the criterion by which a trade is closed out. Exits are even more important than set-ups and entries, but few beginning traders devote much time and effort to studying exits. Trailing stops and profit targets will account for many of the exits you'll make.

A trailing stop is set below the current price for a long position and above the current price for a short position. When you are in a long position, you raise the trailing stop as the market trades higher, locking in profits; while short, you lower the trailing stop as the market trades lower to lock in profits. A trailing stop closes out a long position when prices decline to the trailing stop; a trailing stop closes out a short position when prices advance to the trailing stop.

An alternative to exiting on a trailing stop is exiting at a profit target. A profit target closes out a trade when the price reaches a specified objective. One example of a profit-target exit is to close out a position on the second close above the high of the entry day. Another example is to automatically close out a trade when open profits equal three times the initial risk on the trade. In my own trading, I like to exit half my position at a specified target and to trail a stop on the other half.

One more component of trading that I'd like to discuss is trading psychology. Don't underestimate the importance of psychology to your ultimate trading success. In a sense, it doesn't matter how smart you are or how much you know about systems trading if you can't follow your system with perfect discipline day in and day out. Here's my best advice, most of it learned the hard way, during the past 27 years of trading:

1. If trading seems intimidating at first, remember that you will get used to it by following your system consistently over time. You will not always feel as uncomfortable as you might when you are making your first few trades.

2. Remember that the emotional pain of missing a good trade that your system told you to take is much worse than the pain of losing on a trade that you entered and exited properly, according to your system.

3. Concentrate on learning the business of systems trading and strengthening your ability to follow your system rather than focusing on the dollars gained or lost while you are learning to trade.

4. Don't get overly excited about winning trades or too despondent about losing trades. Maintain equanimity and professionalism. Just follow your system.

5. Congratulate yourself and feel good about a trade when you have done what you were supposed to do according to the rules of your system regardless of the profit or loss on the trade.

6. Remember that learning to trade profitably is a journey not just a destination. The perfect trader does not yet exist. Try to become a better trader each day and enjoy your progress.

As you'll discover, becoming proficient in the use of bar charts is merely the first step for applying technical analysis in the markets. Once you've mastered all the bar chart "basics" - you'll no doubt want to move on to the next phase, and the next. And, most of today's practitioners of technical analysis use the computer as their primary tool, along with one of the popular charting programs now available.

The SuperCharts demo disk included with this booklet will enable you to see how quickly and easily you can put your knowledge of bar charts, moving averages, and momentum oscillators to work. With SuperCharts you can collect data for the markets you want to trade, create bar charts, and apply your favorite indicators to your charts. You can even write, test, and optimize your trading ideas with Omega's EasyLanguage in SuperCharts' QuickEditor. Your adventure in trading can now begin with *Bar Chart Basics* and installation of the SuperCharts demo disk. Enjoy your trading progress — and profits!

— Tom Bierovic
August, 1998

BAR CHART BASICS

Bar Chart Basics

Drop a traditional bar chart in front of almost any novice who doesn't know a thing about trading—even your spouse—and they can probably tell you the trend of prices at a glance. If they can't, odds are pretty good the market is in such a sideways move or congestion phase that it may not be very attractive for you to trade anyway. But, when a market does break out into one of those long extended moves you sometimes see on a chart, even a nontrader can recognize it as an opportunity.

The bar chart is, by far, the most popular method traders use to see how this price action looks. We've already indicated that a bar for any given time period—a minute, a day, a month—shows the high price for the period at the top of the bar, the low price for the period at the bottom of the bar and the closing price at the end of the period indicated by a horizontal line on the right side of the bar. Sometimes the opening price is indicated by a horizontal line on the left side of the price bar. We've also already stated that every factor in the marketplace during the time period the bar—every fundamental, every perception, every fear—is incorporated in that one price bar.

Put a series of these bars for a number of time periods together side by side, and you have a chart. Looking from right to left on a chart, there is no mystery about where the trends or the sideways moves are. They are pretty easy to spot when you look back at past price action. When you look ahead, from left to right, however, it's quite a different matter as you hit the right side of the chart. Technical analysis—the study of price and its action in the past—can help you make some intellectual guesses about the future, but there are no guaranteed answers, no matter how many charts from the past you've examined.

Whole textbooks have been written on bar chart analysis, and many books on trading cover this aspect of technical analysis in some manner. What follows is relatively standard fare on bar chart analysis. It's intended to take some of the mystery out of charting for the beginning technical analyst and provide a basis for discussing charts in other chapters.

For organizational purposes, this chapter will look first at trendlines and continuation patterns and then at reversal formations. You probably wont be surprised to learn that sometimes a pattern can turn out to be either, and it is only in hindsight that you can identify the clues. As with any art, only practice will help you here.

TRENDLINES

"Trade with the trend" is a basic tenet of successful trading. So identifying the trend is where bar chart analysis begins. If a chart does nothing else for you, it is valuable for showing you the trend, even if you are one of those people who remain convinced that a lot of technical analysis is hocus-pocus stuff. For many traders, the trading strategy is simple: As long as the trend is intact, stay with it.

An uptrend is a continuous series of higher highs and higher lows; a downtrend is a series of lower highs and lower lows. To see where a market may be going on a bar chart, connect the lows with a straight line to form the trendline in an uptrend; if the market is going down, draw the trendline across the highs to give you the most important line on the chart.

Nearly every bar chart displays trends of some type. The December crude oil chart has several, most notably the downtrend line (A) from above $19 per barrel in October to below $16 in March and the uptrend line (B) from the low under $15 in late March to well over $19 again in late July (Figure 1 on page 4). Another uptrend line connecting the bottoms in June and July (C) is approximately a 45-degree line, considered to be a significant angle by chartists.

FIGURE 1
SOURCE: OMEGA RESEARCH

Crude Oil, Light 12/94-Daily

The longer the trendline and the more times prices touch it, the more reliable it is and the more "support" it offers the market when prices test it. In a downtrend, the trendline drawn across the descending highs is a point of "resistance"—a line likely to turn back price advances until the market becomes strong enough to break above it as it did here in early April.

The major trendlines on the oil chart have at least three points of contact, as drawn. Remember, chart analysis is an art, and there is some latitude in picking vital points and drawing the lines. Some analysts view the close as the most valuable price and use only closes for trendlines, ignoring the highs or lows that define the trendline points for other analysts. That would give slightly different levels of support and resistance and a little different view on where the breakouts occur. That's part of the art of chart analysis.

The first spurt away from the bottom produces a steep short-term trendline on the crude oil chart, typical as a market breaks out of an old trend. But the steeper the trendline, the harder it is to maintain, and the market quickly settles into a steadier, sustainable climb. Once trendline B is broken, you could establish another trendline at a lower level (D) as a support area once a new low seems to be in place. This low, by the way, can be projected as we'll explain in the retracement discussion below.

Another feature of a trendline on bar charts is that a parallel line (E) often develops and produces a well-defined "chan-

FIGURE 2
SOURCE: OMEGA RESEARCH

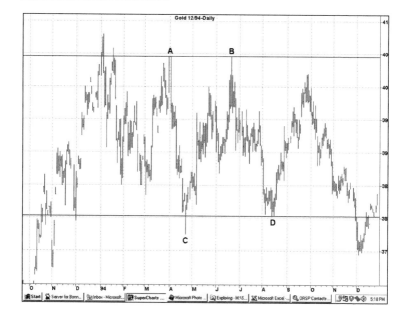
Gold 12/94-Daily

nel," a relatively narrow band of price action within two parallel trendlines. Once a channel is established, close followers of the market might use "breakouts" of the channel to establish positions: A break above the top of the uptrend channel would suggest an even stronger market than has existed, offering a buy opportunity; a break below the channel indicates weakness and a possible sell signal.

Or you might assume after a while chat the most likely course of action is for prices to stay within the channel: Buy when prices approach the bottom of the channel, sell when they get near the top of the channel. Stay alert for channel breakouts, however.

Another type of "trend" or "channel" formation is a sideways move. December gold futures prices stayed within a $25 per oz, channel for much of 1934, including weeks on end in a range of less than $10 (Figure 2). Tops (A and B) and bottoms (C and D) seem to have the market confined between about $380 and $405 per oz. Traders who are convinced this is a sideways market use the top of the channel or trading range to sell and the bottom to buy, assuming the market will reverse its course at those resistance and support points to stay within the range whenever either trendline is tested.

The width of the channel will help you determine whether this is a viable strategy to trade. The $25 range in gold equals $2,500 per contract, an amount you might find worth pursuing if you capture only part of a move. In some cases, the range is so narrow that your account could get chewed up by gyrations within the channel, even when you've determined correctly what type of market it is. For example, cattle futures traded sideways within about a half-cent range or only $200 per contract for weeks in 1394. It's difficult to get positioned in a market like that and is not an attractive situation for any trader except perhaps for someone who wants to sell options.

Lackluster as it may seem to be, you need to watch a sideways formation especially carefully: The longer a market moves sideways, the more energy it tends to store up. When the market breaks out from a double, triple or multiple top or bottom of a trading range, the pent-up energy can produce a significant move in the direction of the breakout.

CONTINUATION FORMATIONS

If the first thing you look for on a bar chart is the trend, your second question probably will be something like, "Okay, there's the trend. Now, will it continue or reverse!" Your logical follow-up questions might be, "And, if the trend continues, how long or how far will it continue! If the trend reverses, how far or how long will the reversal be!" Technical analysis will give you some clues, but keep in mind that this is a subjective art and the answers are not absolute.

Markets seldom go straight up or down. In most cases, a trend will be interrupted by "congestion areas," "pauses" or "resting periods" as prices react against the main trend, per-

haps for days or even a few weeks. As bears and bulls sort out
the dominant psychological force in the marketplace, chart patterns may develop that suggest a turn in direction or a continuation of the larger trend already in place. Even when a trend
remains intact, you may find countertrend moves you want to
trade, depending on your trading style.

Bar chart patterns that suggest a move will continue include
"symmetrical triangles" or "pennants," "ascending triangles"
and "descending triangles" and "flags." Sometimes one formation will evolve into another. You can see some examples of
these patterns on the same crude oil chart as we used to show
trendlines (to reduce clutter, the major trendlines aren't
shown). These aren't the only examples of formations on these
charts nor even the best—your eye may pick out some others.

The names pretty well describe how the formations look.
Much depends on where these patterns occur on the overall
chart picture. With triangles in general, prices tend to trade in
a narrower and narrower range or coil before springing out
with another strong move. The evidence of such a formation is
more conclusive if the level of trading volume generally follows
the same pattern as the level of prices. CAUTION: A breakout
may not be in the direction of the prevailing trend; triangles
also can be reversal formations.

The breakout of an ascending or descending triangle that
develops during a trend usually is through the flat side of the
triangle (A, B, C, E, H on oil chart, figure 3 on page 11). In a

descending triangle, prices are pressed down to the baseline several times and rally less each time until they break below the baseline. After the break, prices frequently come back to the baseline to retest it, but it may become the new ceiling (in a descending triangle) or support floor (in an ascending triangle) as it turns back prices. This is the adjustment period for traders as they start to accept a new price level.

A pennant or symmetrical triangle reflects uncertainty and a time for traders to pause and catch up with the market. A series of lower highs and higher lows winds chart action into a tight little coil pattern at the apex of the triangle. When the market springs out of the pennant, the breakout often comes on a wide range day and in the same direction as the trend leading into the pennant. This is one of the more reliable chart patterns.

A flag formation is a short-term trend against the prevailing trend—a bear flag with lower highs and lower lows in a larger bullish trend (F and G on the crude oil chart) or a bull flag with higher lows and higher highs in an overall bearish move (I on the crude oil chart). The best examples come after a sharp move that actually looks like a "flagpole" on which to anchor the flag (G is a better example than F on the oil chart). The market seems to need a rest for a bit to sort out what it's done after making a quick spurt up or down and, in effect, is assessing whether the move is real. Once it has consolidated its forces, it is ready for the next phase of its original trend.

FIGURE 3
Source: Omega Research

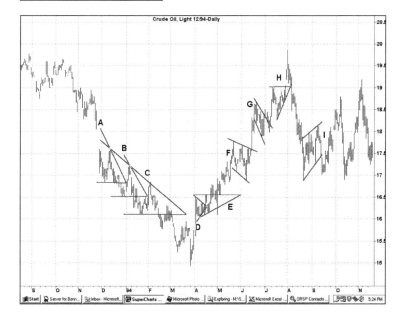

Crude Oil, Light 12/94-Daily

MEASURING A CONTINUATION TREND

Anticipating a question you may have at this point: Yes, it is possible to read too much into a bar chart and to imagine a pattern that coincides with or reinforces your market bias. As market action is unfolding, it frankly is often very difficult to determine the current chart pattern. Price action on the crude oil chart after H looks a lot like earlier action on the chart, but it turned out to be a top (at least for the time shown) while action at D, E, E and G developed into triangles and flags that continued the uptrend.

When you're in the middle of F, it is difficult to recognize it as a flag and not a potential top. However, don't give up on technical analysis at this point. As this formation develops, you get several valuable pieces of information:

1. Early in the countertrend move, it's not clear what will happen. If you had a eight uptrend line drawn on the April-May lows, you may even have been stopped out of a long position when prices dropped below the trendline in the third week of the counter move. As the countertrend price points became evident—first a low, then a lower high, then a lower low—a flag began to look like a possibility but still wasn't a foregone conclusion.

Even without knowing what the emerging formation was, however, you at least had logical places to put stops, no matter what happened-a buy stop at the upper line, a sell stop below the lower line or the low

point of the countertrend. You may have had an opin-
ion about the next move based on your other analysis,
but on the bar chart evidence alone, you still don't
know whether this is a flag in an overall uptrend or the
top of the uptrend after three weeks. All you do know
is that your stops can put you in a position to get
onboard a move in either direction.

2. Once the breakout above the top line has occurred
and your stop has gotten you long, analysis of what is
evidently a flag formation can give you a clue about a
second important item of concern— how far the
uptrend might continue. This is not an exact science
either, but formations such as pennants and flags
tend to occur about halfway through a move. The
"length" of the flagpole also can be used to project
the next move.

Look at the crude oil chart again (Figure 4 on page 14),
beginning with the pennant/symmetrical triangle labeled D on
the previous chart. The flagpole created by the upward spike
off the bottom measures about 160 points (vertical line J). Add
that amount to the breakout point at $16.30 per barrel near
the apex of the triangle, and you get a target of $17.90 (vertical
line K). After prices break above triangle D, they fall back to
retest the area and then almost drop below the triangle lows in
early May before moving up nearly to the target projected by
the symmetrical triangle.

Similarly the less well-defined flagpole leading into the flag
formation F measures about 175 points (vertical line L). Added
to the point where prices break out above the flag, the projec-

FIGURE 4
SOURCE: OMEGA RESEARCH

Crude Oil, Light 12/94-Daily

tion is for a high around $19.30 (vertical line M). Likewise, the 125-point flagpole for flag formation G (vertical line N) sets a target for the high above $19.50 (vertical line O).

The concept can be applied to the downside as well. The slide from the top to the beginning of what appears to be a bear flag formation (I) covers approximately 300 points (vertical line P). Subtract that amount from the point where prices break out below the bottom of the flag, and the projected low is in the $14.50 vicinity (vertical line Q). Likely! At the time of the breakout in September, all you could say is that, based on technical analysis studies of flag formations in the past, that's what it looked like. A month later, you might wonder whether you even had a flag formation (Figure 5).

FIGURE 5
SOURCE: OMEGA RESEARCH

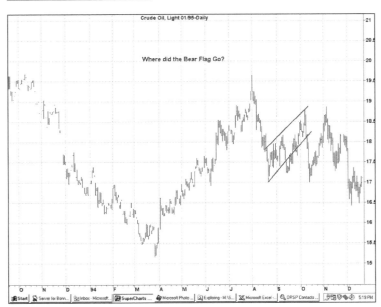

You can do similar calculations with ascending and descending triangles. Figure our the difference between the high and the base (support area) of a descending triangle and subtract that figure from the base to get a downtrend target after prices break below the base. In an ascending triangle, find the difference between the low at the start of the triangle and the baseline (resistance area) and add that amount to the baseline to get an upside target after prices break above the baseline.

MEASURING GAPS

Another continuation formation amounts to nothing-that is, there actually is no formation but a "gap" or a price level where no trading takes place in a running market. This can be a "measuring gap."

To a fundamentalist, that's a point at which something so dramatic has happened that no one wants any part of the market at the current price level. The supply or demand situation has changed so drastically that prices jump to a totally new level with no buying or selling at the intervening prices.

To a technician, a measuring gap performs somewhat the same function as a pennant or symmetrical triangle, typically marking the halfway point in a move between a bottom and top or vice versa. The most visible gap on the crude oil chart is the unusually large gap in November (Figure 4 on page 14). Prices had been near $20 and were close to $18 at the time of the gap-a $2 drop. To calculate an objective based on this measuring gap, subtract $2 from the bottom of the gap- $17.50 minus $2 puts a downside target in the $15.50 area.

As you might expect in this subjective world, gaps are fairly common on bar charts, and not every gap means something. Some measuring gaps may turn out to be exhaustion gaps that indicate a reversal, not a continuation, of the trend. Bur a correctly diagnosed measuring gap can be helpful in projecting a price objective.

REVERSAL FORMATIONS

Like a surfer looking for the big wave, the chart traders dream is to catch a big trend early and stay onboard for a long ride. That would seem to be relatively easy to do when you look at a bar chart in hindsight. But, as we have already mentioned, what looks like a continuation formation may turn into a reversal signal instead. When the big one does come along, it may not look that attractive initially and traders often find it hard to catch the wave.

As the previous section indicated, price patterns along the way sometimes suggest a move will continue and even offer clues about how far it could go. Obviously, however, trends do not continue forever. What you need are signals that tell you when one trend is ending and another is beginning so you can establish a new position or exit an old one if you have been riding a trend. Technical analysis also reveals those signals, but, again, remember the caveat: Chart analysis is an art and not a science. It is quite likely not all traders will read a chart precisely the same way.

To discover reversal patterns, you'll have to start at exactly the same place as you do for finding continuation patterns—the trend revealed by the trendline, the straight line drawn across the bottoms of price action as an uptrend records a series of higher lows and higher highs or, if it is a downtrend, the straight line drawn across the tops as the market establishes lower highs and lower lows.

As long as the integrity of a trendline is maintained, the trend continues, and position traders may find it risky to go against the trend. In the battle between market bulls and bears, a trendline often becomes a crucial support/resistance factor in determining whether a trend will continue or reverse. The more a trendline is tested and the more points of contact on the trendline, the stronger it is. But all trendlines are penetrated at some point. When that happens, what had been support often becomes stout resistance and vice versa.

Breaking a trendline is the simplest, most basic chart reversal pattern. It could be a false move or a trap, of course, but a trendline break usually signals some new market action you need to watch—a new trend in the opposite direction, a pause or short-term congestion in the direction of the longer trend or perhaps just a shift to a sideways market.

If the crude oil chart here looks familiar, it should: It is the same chart used earlier in the chapter to show continuation patterns (Figure 6 on page 20). After trending down for nearly six months (A), crude oil prices finally bolted above the downtrend line with several wide-range days, forming the "flagpole" that was discussed above in the section on continuation formations. Then, after trending upward for four months, prices broke below the major uptrend lines (B and C), again with wide-range days. It may look almost too simple, but penetrating trendlines of such duration is one of the most significant bar chart reversal formations.

RETRACEMENTS

One subject that needs to be interjected here is the matter of "retracements" or "corrections."

When a trendline has been broken and a new trend begun, chart analysts naturally would like to have a way to project how far the new trend might go and at what point might this new trend be reversed. The section on market structure will go into this topic in more detail, especially in the discussion of Fibonacci numbers and ratios, bur this is an important item to introduce here because it is a key part of the analysis of either the continuation or the reversal pattern.

Every time the market acts, it usually reacts, the amount of the reaction depending upon the market's strength or weakness. A flag is an example of a relatively minor reaction against the main trend action as a move continues on its way.

FIGURE 6

SOURCE: OMEGA RESEARCH

Perhaps the most common possibility for a reaction observed on a number of bar charts is a 50 percent retracement or a "correction" that takes back 50 percent of the market's previous move (Figure 7 on page 22). There is no magic about 50 percent—some use eighths of a previous move or Fibonacci ratios or Gann techniques—but this is a chart point where experience tells some analysts to expect new support or new resistance to turn the new, shorter trend around.

The major uptrend on the crude oil chart took prices up about $5 per barrel from a little below $15 to almost $20. After prices gave up 25 percent of that move and broke below the major uptrend lines, analysts might look to a 50 percent retracement as the next possible level for support. Also note that the pause (flag I) in the downtrend developed at about the same price level as the pause (flag F) in the uptrend about three months earlier.

Retracement levels can be a clue to continuation or reversal pattern targets. Another related possibility for calculating either a continuation or reversal target is the "measuring gap," discussed above as a continuation pattern because it usually occurs about halfway through a move. If the gap on the crude oil chart at the $17.50–$18 area is a measuring gap, we have already mentioned the continuation pattern's objective would be the $15.50 vicinity—not only the objective for that major move but also the place to watch for the next major turn. One traders continuation clue may be the basis for another's reversal prediction.

FIGURE 7
SOURCE: OMEGA RESEARCH

In addition, the measuring gap can also provide a reversal target of another type. Gaps sometimes are tough to "fill"— that is, getting price action to take place at the level where no buying or selling occurred earlier. As markets struggle to get through a gap area, the gap itself sometimes acts as a support or resistance area. Because the measuring gap, by definition, is at the 50 percent retracement level, there may be a couple of arguments for expecting at least some reversal action at this point in the ensuing April-July uptrend, as is suggested by the flag/pause labeled F on the crude oil chart.

KEY REVERSAL

One chart feature that is mentioned often in market commentaries is a "key reversal"—in an uptrend, a market drives to new highs and then closes on or near the low and below the previous period's low; in a downtrend, the market hits new lows and then turns around to close on or near the high and above the previous period's high. While they may be popular in technical trader talk, the problem is key reversals are not very reliable. Some would say they are no better than 50-50 in projecting actual turns.

ISLAND REVERSAL

An "island reversal," which may take several days to develop, tends to be a more reliable bar chart reversal pattern. The price action in an island reversal formation is isolated from what happens before or after that period and usually stands out on a bar chart (Figure 8).

FIGURE 8
SOURCE: OMEGA RESEARCH

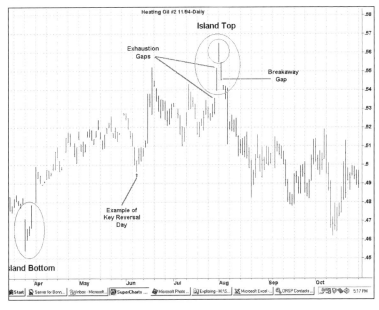

On the left side going into the formation is an "exhaustion gap," a price level where no trading rakes place as traders seem to put everything into one last gasp to continue the trend. The "island" is a bar or several bars that push to a new high or low before closing on a low or high. On the right side is a "breakaway gap," a familiar sight as a market begins to move away from the previous trend and picks up steam, sometimes almost appearing to panic to get away from the old price level.

The crude oil chart we have been using almost produced that type of pattern at the very bottom and the very top. The pattern shows up more clearly on the heating oil chart.

MULTIPLE TOPS, BOTTOMS

Another marker axiom suggests, "Sell double or triple tops; buy double or triple bottoms." That assumes, of course, that the concept of support/resistance is driving the market. In that case, whenever prices approach the previous tops or the top of a channel or sideways market, sell; whenever prices approach the previous bottoms or the bottom of a channel or sideways move, buy.

Look back at the gold chart in the continuation formation section (page 6). Selling at A and B and buying at C and D look like good moves, creating the extremes of the channel as reversal targets. But what do you do on the next thrust to a channel line! Will it be the one that breaks out and turns everything around' One approach is that, until a market proves otherwise, treat the shorter moves as reversal opportunities. However, as we cautioned above, you need to be especially nimble if you want to trade these situations: A breakout from a side-ways pattern can produce an explosive move in either direction, and what was an extended continuation pattern can become a big reversal move. This is where your money management skills become most important.

Vs AND SAUCERS

Some volatile markets tend to spike up or down and then react in the opposite direction almost immediately in a reversal action that looks like a "V" on a bar chart (Figure 9). Others seem to take forever to establish what look like rounding or saucer tops or bottoms. It's hard to catch a V top or bottom, and the saucer top or bottom may be so slow in developing that it will try any traders patience.

The silver chart features plenty of V-type reversal formations as prices race up and down $3,000 per contract several times within a few weeks. The crude oil chart bottom and top also look like Vs. You have to know your market and use other aspects of technical analysis to get good positions in these types of markets.

On the other hand, copper moved gently lower and then higher over a period of several months before it came out of its rounding bottom (Figure 10 on page 28). Note that as the market moved above the right lip of the saucer, it left a gap as it jumped to higher ground and never looked back.

HEAD-AND-SHOULDERS

Perhaps it's just the name that makes it memorable, but "head-and-shoulders" tops or bottoms are among the best-known chart reversal formations. Sometimes traders stretch to see a head-and-shoulders, and a picture-perfect one is hard to

FIGURE 9
SOURCE: OMEGA RESEARCH

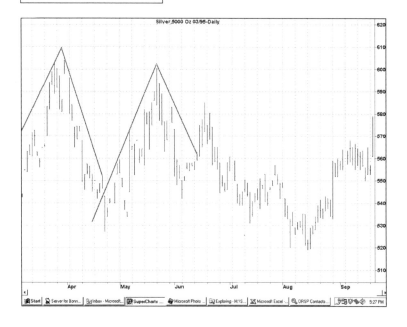

FIGURE 1 0
SOURCE: OMEGA RESEARCH

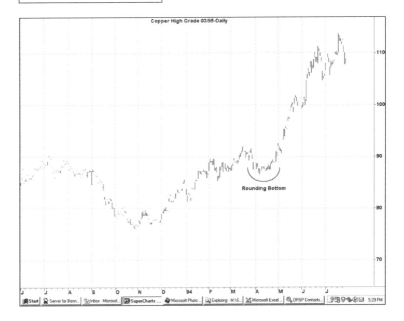

find. However, when a real head-and-shoulders shows up on a chart, the breaking of a "neckline" does tend to provide a good indication the market will follow through in the direction of the breakout.

In a head-and-shoulders top, the market drives to a high and then reacts downward in what may be a flag continuation formation to form the "left shoulder." Then it propels itself back up to a new high to form the "head." As prices fall to complete the head, they hit a low reasonably in line with the bottom of the move between the left shoulder and the head. Then the market reacts higher again in what may be another flag formation to form the "right shoulder." The top of the right shoulder is somewhat close to the top of the left shoulder but not as high as the head.

The neckline connecting the two lows formed by the shoulders is the key point. As prices move down from the right shoulder and penetrate below this neckline, that's the signal to sell. Some analysts measure the distance from the top of the head to the neckline and project that the bottom will be the same distance below the neckline.

To be a true head-and-shoulders, the formation should come at the end of an extended move, and the pattern of trading volume should be roughly the same as the pattern of prices.

FIGURE 11
SOURCE: OMEGA RESEARCH

FIGURE 12
SOURCE: OMEGA RESEARCH

The head-and-shoulders isn't always pretty or exact, as the examples illustrate (Figures 11 and 12). On the daily cocoa chart, the left shoulder is a little messy, the head includes a double top, and the neckline is at quite an angle in version 1. But, when the neckline is broken, the price action is what you would expect for a head-and-shoulders. If you "see" the chart a little differently, you might make out another version of a head-and-shoulders with a more horizontal neckline (Figure 12). This is just one example of how subjective chart analysis can be.

Using this reversal formation to project a low after the breakout, measure the distance from the top of the head to the neckline and subtract that figure from the point where the breakout of the neckline occurs. On version 1 of the daily cocoa chart, that puts the bottom target at $1,260 per metric ton. Version 2 would put the bottom projection below $1,100, which coincides with the previous bottoms.

The weekly cocoa chart gives you another look at the head-and-shoulders formation in the making (Figure 13). It reveals that the earlier bottoms comprised the neckline of what had all the appearances of being another head-and-shoulders top, but it failed to complete the breaking of the neckline. Sometimes

FIGURE 13
SOURCE: OMEGA RESEARCH

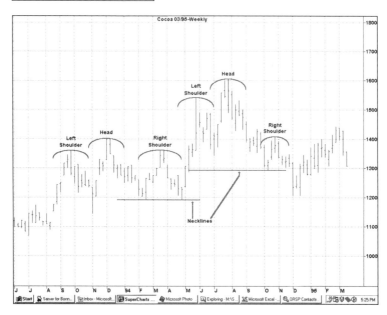

FIGURE 14
SOURCE: OMEGA RESEARCH

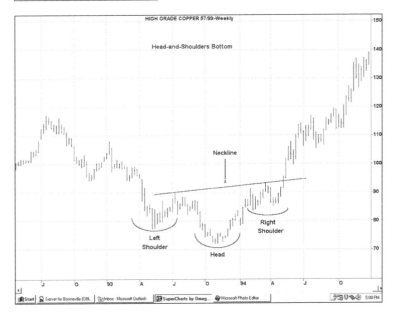

you may "see" such obvious formations shaping up, but you need to remain flexible. One advantage of chart analysis is that, even when your formation "fails" to materialize, you can use it to gauge market sentiment and develop appropriate trading strategies for the new conditions. On the cocoa chart, failure of a possible head-and-shoulders to follow through to lower levels indicated a stronger market and higher prices.

The weekly copper chart shows that the same principles of a top apply to head-and-shoulders bottoms (Figure 14).

Ms AND Ws, 1-2-3 SWINGS

"M" tops and "W" bottoms that aren't perfect can also be reliable chart reversal patterns. They look quite similar to the double tops or bottoms described above, but the right side of the letter doesn't extend as far as the left side. Ms and Ws also resemble the head-and-shoulders formation but are missing a shoulder. Some analysts identify this formation as a 1-2-3 swing and have based advisory services on tactics for trading these swings.

In an M top such as on the weekly T-bond chart (Figure 15), prices hit a high, drop to a reaction low (1), rally back to a high that is not quite as high as the previous high (2) and then fall

FIGURE 15
SOURCE: OMEGA RESEARCH

again. When prices drop below the reaction low, that's the signal to sell (3), placing a stop at the secondary high (2).

In this case, two Ms have been superimposed at the top on the chart, using the virtual double top at 122 for the tops of the M for one and combining these two tops into one broader top on a larger M. On the larger M, the slide to below 114 is the reaction low ①, and the weak bounce to 117 is the secondary high ②. The sell signal (or the place to have a sell stop) occurs when prices fall below the reaction low ① under 114 again ③. Once short, the protective stop would be placed at about 118 above the secondary high ②.

When the high at 2 goes higher than the previous high or if 3 does not drop below 1, you negate the M formation and come up with a different plan. A top and an M appeared to be forming in the first half of 1993 (dashed lines) on the weekly T-bond chart. However, your sell stop below the reaction low around 108 ☐1 would not have been activated as prices in a possible leg ☐3 did not go below the reaction low ☐1. In fact, as prices moved above the secondary high ☐2, it looked more like a W bottoming formation, and your stop might have been a buy stop instead above the secondary high.

The same 1-2-3 count principles apply to a W bottom: Prices on the daily Kansas City wheat chart (Figure 16) drive to a low, bounce back to a reaction high (1), drop off again but not below the first low (2) and then move up above the reaction high (1), providing a buy signal (3). Once long, the protective sell stop is placed below the secondary low (2).

FIGURE 16
SOURCE: OMEGA RESEARCH

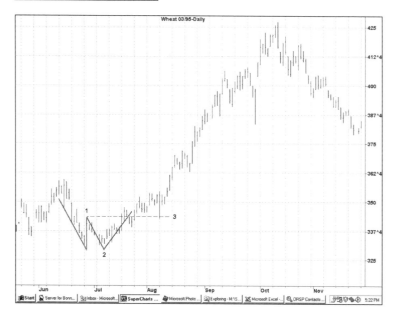

RETESTS

Whenever prices penetrate a trendline or the boundaries of a chart formation, note that the market often comes back to the key breakout lines and points to retest them before taking off. This are-you-really- sure-you-want-to-do-this action quite often gives you several opportunities to position yourself at the breakout point, but it also can be a tricky area to trade. Market action may become more volatile as traders react differently to the breakout. Or it may spiral into congestion as the market sorts out what it wants to do. Either way, price action at significant breakouts often is enough to try a traders patience—and bank account.

Sometimes the best-laid plans of the technical analyst work like a charm. But, remember, this is an art, not an exact science. That's the dilemma you face when you're operating at the hard right edge of the chart without the benefit of hindsight.

About the Author

DARRELL JOBMAN is a freelance writer, editorial consultant and trader in Waterloo, Iowa. His extensive experience in agricultural and commodity oriented publications includes 21 years at Oster Communications, where he was the editor-in-chief of *Futures* magazine. He continues to be involved in editorial projects and trader conferences, and has done editorial work for the Futures Industry Association. He is the author of *The Handbook of Technical Analysis.*

TOM BIEROVIC is manager of system trading and development education at Omega Research, Inc. He is well known for seminars he has presented on system trading and developement in over 35 countries and six continents. He has been profiled and interviewed in both *Futures* and *Technical Analysis of Stocks & Commodities* magazines. *Playing for Keeps*, Tom's new book, will be available through Traders' Library.

Trading
Resource
Guide

❖

Tools for Success
in Trading

If you own *Bar Chart Basics* ... Deduct $20 when you purchase Darrell Jobman's *THE HANDBOOK OF TECHNICAL ANALYSIS**

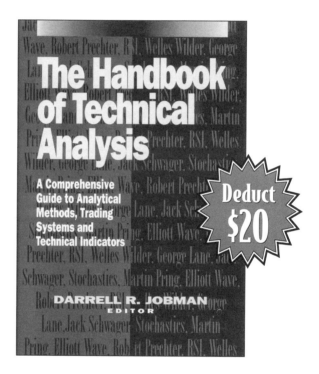

Mastering the "bar chart basics" is just the first step for applying technical analysis to forecast the markets. Darrell Jobman - author of *Bar Chart Basics* - has also written the most comprehensive, definitive reference course on the topic - *The Handbook of Technical Analysis*.

*Deduction cannot be used in conjunction with any other discount coupons or programs.

This sweeping work features contributions by some of the top minds in technical analysis - from Jack Schwager and Tom DeMark to Robert Prechter, Bill Williams, Welles Wilder — and more.

And, as a *Bar Chart Basics* owner, you are can DEDUCT $20 from the price of this industry "Bible."

You'll find in-depth coverage of ...

· **Charts:** Going beyond bar charts - learn everything from point & figure and candlesticks to Market Profile - in clear, simple terms.

· **Indicators:** Moving averages, RSI, Oscillators, stochastics, sequentials and more - everything you need to monitor price movement.

· **Sentiment:** Discover how to assess the underlying sentiment of the market - and use it to your advantage.

· **Structure:** Cycles, seasonal patterns and other natural patterns found in studies of R.N. Elliott, Fibonacci and W.D. Gann - learn the strengths and weaknesses of the leading structural approaches.

Move on to the next level with
THE HANDBOOK OF TECHNICAL ANALYSIS
... and SAVE $20!

The Handbook of Technical Analysis

Deduct $20

ORDER TODAY! CALL 1-800-272-2855 EXT T193
OR FAX THIS FORM TO 410-964-0027

Name: _____

Address: _____

City: _____ St/Pr: _____ Zip/Postal: _____

Item #3419 The Handbook of Technical Analysis
$55.00 - $20.00=$35 + $4.95 Shipping = $39.95

Card #:_____ expires:_____

SUGGESTED READING LIST

THE HANDBOOK OF TECHNICAL ANALYSIS, *Darrell Jobman, editor,*
In-depth look at all aspects of technical analysis. The roster of contributors is a
"Who's Who" of trading: Wilder on RSI, Schwager on the uses & abuses of technical analysis, Pring on momentum, Prechter on Elliott Wave and more. From
bar charts to candlesticks, volume to Gann - it's a #1 guide to the profit-grabbing
techniques of the masters. 400 PP $55.00 ITEM #3419

THE VISUAL INVESTOR-, *John Murphy,* Track the ups & downs of stock
prices by visually comparing charts - instead of relying on complex formulas and
technical concepts. Introduces readers to Intermarket Analysis - a proven analyti-
cal approach based on evaluating the impact different markets have on each
other. 256 PP $39.95 ITEM #2379

MARTIN PRING'S INTRODUCTION TO TECHNICAL ANALYSIS, *Martin J.
Pring,* The foremost expert on technical analysis and forecasting financial
markets gives you a one-on-one course in every aspect of technical analysis. This
interactive guide explains how to evaluate trends, highs & lows, price/volume
relationships, price patterns, moving averages, and momentum indicators.

The accompanying CD-ROM includes videos, animated diagrams, audio clips and
interactive tests. It's the user-friendly way to master technical analysis from an
industry icon. 303 PP $49.95 ITEM #8521

ANALYZING BAR CHARTS FOR PROFIT, *John Magee,* A straightforward
guide teaching the time-tested approach of using technical analysis to minimize
risk and boost profits. You'll learn: classical chart patterns; how to identify
trends & trading ranges, tops bottoms and what these terms mean to your bottom
line. Plus the "Magee Method" of buying/selling, and editorials from Magee's
market letters. It's the best "explanation of the technical process ever written."

224 PP $39.95 ITEM #2318

To order any book listed and receive a special
15% "TRADE SECRETS" Discount
Call 1-800-272-2855 ext. T193

TECHNICAL ANALYSIS OF STOCK TRENDS, *7th Edition, Edwards & Magee,* A universally acclaimed classic, updated with the latest data in market performance and trends, on which the foundation of all technical analysis is built. Step-by-step coverage thoroughly explains and applies the current data. Stochastics, trendlines, stops, reversals, support/resistance and tactical usage of each.   704 PP $75.00 ITEM #2376

TECHNICAL ANALYSIS OF THE FUTURES MARKETS, *John Murphy,* This Bible of technical analysis for all markets details every major technical tool used to chart the markets in concise, practical terms. Complex indicators are described in understandable terms. You'll learn it all - from CNBC's Tech Talk host: stochastics, price patterns, RSI, volume, Elliott wave, Gann, cycles, etc.

570 PP $59.95 ITEM #2366

Study Guide
Reinforce and perfect what you've learned from Murphy's classic text. Reviews and exercises on actual charts help you retain material covered in the book.

$29.95 ITEM #2368

POINT & FIGURE CHARTING, *Thomas J. Dorsey,* Now, the first new work on Point & Figure in 30 years. Today's leading expert shows how to use point and figure to chart price movements on stocks, options, futures and mutual funds. Learn to interpret the point and figure charts and recognize patterns that signal outstanding opportunities. Also covers how to combine point and figure with technical analysis for unbeatable success. You can't afford to pass by this valuable trading tool - & Dorsey makes it easier than ever.

304 PP $59.95 ITEM #2364

STOCK PATTERNS FOR DAY TRADING, *Barry Rudd,* Profit from short term and intraday price swings with the winning methods this professional stock trader reveals. Intraday trend trades, scalps, swing trades - it's all here. Great for novices and can help all traders improve their skills.

224 PP $95.00 ITEM #8855

THE ARMS INDEX (TRIN INDEX), *Richard Arms, Jr.,* Finally, it's
updated and back in print! Get an in depth look at how volume - not time - governs market price changes. Describes the Arms' short-term trading index (TRIN), a measure of the relative strength of the volume in relation to advancing stocks against that of declines. Also shows how to use Arms' own system to forecast the price changes of individual issues as well as market indexes. A true trading gem.

100 PP $39.95 ITEM #3130

NEW MARKET TIMING TECHNIQUES, *Thomas R. DeMark,* He's a
"trading system developer without peer," says Futures magazine. Now' DeMark stakes out new territory while refining the most popular and precise of his indicators. With a focus on real-time trading applications, he also reveals - for the first time - complete details of a new indicator: the TD combo. This potent new tool for understanding market rhythms and calculating buy/sell opportunities is introduced in full detail. Don't miss it.

288 PP $69.95 ITEM #5712

TECHNICAL ANALYSIS AND STOCK MARKET PROFITS, *Richard*
Schabacker, Everyone from Edwards & Magee on consider this classic the foundation on which all technical analysis is built. It examines patterns, formations, trends, support and resistance areas, etc - which comprise the basis of modern technical analysis, from the "Grandfather" of it all, and the former finance editor at Forbes and the New York Times.

470 PP $65.00 ITEM #8473

IMPORTANT INTERNET SITES

TRADERS' LIBRARY BOOKSTORE — *www.traderslibrary.com,* the #1 source for trading and investment books, videos and related products.

OMEGA RESEARCH — *www.omegaresearch.com,* Information on Omega products, support, and solution providers. Also listing of their free seminars.

PC QUOTE — *www.pcquote.com,* The premier source for free quotes and charts.

DORSEY WRIGHT — *www.dorseywright.com,* The source for information on Point & Figure analysis and comprehensive Point & Figure charts.

EQUITY ANALYTICS — *www.e-analytics.com,* An excellent educational resource with extensive glossaries for technical analysis and many other topics.

MURPHYMORRIS — *www.murphymorris.com,* The site of Technical Analysis Gurus John Murphy and Greg Morris. A perfect site for both beginners and those more experienced in Technical Analysis

WALL STREET DIRECTORY — *www.wsdinc.com,* The best directory of financial sites on the web. A comprehensive source that will help you find the answers to your financial questions.

DOW JONES SEMINARS — *www.seminarsdowjones.com,* The site of the best technical analysis conference around. Get a speaker list, registration information and a schedule for this 20 year old conference.

JOE KRUTSINGER — *www.joekrut.com,* The site of the author of this book and expert system developer. Includes information on his systems with information on how to get them.

WALL STREET DIRECTORY — *www.wsdinc.com,* The best directory of financial sites on the web. A comprehensive source that will help you find the answers to your financial questions.

FUTURES TRUTH — *www.futurestruth.com,* Independantly tracks hundreds of publicly available commodity trading systems.

FUTURES MAGAZINE — *www.futuresmag.com,* Filled with information for futures traders as well as books, videos, and information about their conferences.

SUPERCHARTS

FREE
30-DAY TRIAL

Disk included with this book

The reason is clear: *Designed from the ground up for Microsoft Windows, SuperCharts provides more analysis power than any other technical analysis program ever developed for the individual investor. Plus it's amazingly easy to learn and use. By combining powerful system testing and automation features with state-of-the-art charting, SuperCharts provides the professionals' choice for finding, improving and tracking custom trading strategies that make money.*

It includes a Windows 95 interface, full-color charting, a built-in data downloader and an expert system that reveals what each of the 80+ indicators are saying about a symbol at any point in time. With the ability to write custom indicators, studies and systems with built-in buy and sell alerts and scan each chart for a different set of conditions, it's the perfect tool for analyzing all markets to discover the potential profit-makers quickly and easily.

And now with both an end-of-day and a real-time version of SuperCharts available, you can follow the markets in the time frame that best suits your own trading needs.

"SuperCharts 4 is an exciting breakthrough that puts the insights of professional market analysts in the hands of the average investor."

-John Murphy, Host of *CNBC's Tech Talk*, July '96

"SuperCharts End of Day is an amazing product...does an excellent job of making charting quick and easy...an excellent program with excellent service."

-Courtney Smith, *Commodity Traders Consumers Reports*, August 1996

"3 1/2 Disks,"-*Futures* Magazine

"SuperCharts 3.0 is designed to be easy, efficient and, with the use of the CD for a database, your best opportunity for trading today...I was impressed with SuperCharts 3.0 and I think you will be too."

-Thom Hartle, *Technical Analysis of Stocks & Commodities*, October '95

BONUS
Order the full version of
SuperCharts for $395
and receive a $20
Traders' Library Gift
Certificate

To order call
800-439-8016 *ask for extension 4091c*
or 305-551-9991 *ask for extension 4091c*

OPTIONSTATION 1.2

Imagine

knowing which options positions offer the most profit potential according to your market outlook...all in a matter of seconds. Imagine using the same proven options trading strategies as some of the world's most successful options traders when making your own investment decisions...and not having to spend years learning how to put them to work. Imagine being able to determine whether an option is overvalued or undervalued...

with just a click of your mouse.

OptionStation is the first and only options analysis software for Windows® that helps you find and track the most profitable options positions available based on your own market assumptions. It's designed to sort through thousands of possible option positions and uncover those that offer the greatest chance of making money based on any user-defined assumptions. Then it even allows you to follow those positions in real-time, delayed or end-of-day basis and work with "what if..." scenarios, allowing you to observe the different risk/reward results associated with each one. In essence, it unleashes the awesome analysis power of your PC in your search for winning option strategies. And best of all it's easy enough for a beginner to be up and running in no time at all...

Never again will you have to blindly risk your valuable capital. Or limit yourself to only very basic options trades. Or even wonder what option positions are best suited to your market objectives. All because of the amazing capabilities of OptionStation.

Futures Software Review Honors OptionStation With Highest Rating
-- *Four Disks*

"It is surely a testament to the age we live in that a package like OptionStation 1.2 is available: The recommended system requirements, common now, were simply unthinkable for the mass market only five years ago. Omega Research, which has developed products such as TradeStation and SuperCharts, has made some impressive strides in simplifying the complexity of options trading for a less-technical audience," stated Howard L. Simons, Contributing Writer of *Futures*.

You can purchase OptionStation for 12 monthly payments of $149.95 with 0% APR, plus a one-time, non-refundable $19.95 shipping and handling fee. OptionStation includes SuperCharts Real-Time absolutely free, or you can get an $840 credit towards the price of TradeStation.

To order call
800-439-8016 *ask for extension 4091c*
or 305-551-9991 *ask for extension 4091c*

BONUS: Order OptionStation and receive a $50 Traders' Library Gift Certificate

This book, along with other books, are available at discounts that make it realistic to provide them as gifts to your customers, clients, and staff. For more information on these long lasting, cost effective premiums, please call John Boyer at 800-424-4550 or email him at john@traderslibrary.com.

THIS CD IS EQUIPPED WITH AN AUTORUN FEATURE. SIMPLY PLACE IT IN THE CD-ROM DRIVE AND IT WILL INSTALL. IF THE AUTORUN FEATURE DOES NOT EXECUTE, SELECT START FROM THE WINDOWS 95 TOOLBAR, RUN, D:(OR YOUR CD-ROM DRIVE LETTER)SCDEMO.EXE